The
ROALD DAHL
QUIZBOOK

Books by Roald Dahl

THE BFG
BOY: TALES OF CHILDHOOD
CHARLIE AND THE CHOCOLATE FACTORY
CHARLIE AND THE CHOCOLATE FACTORY: A Play
CHARLIE AND THE GREAT GLASS ELEVATOR
CHARLIE AND THE GREAT GLASS ELEVATOR: A Play
THE COMPLETE ADVENTURES OF CHARLIE AND MR
   WILLY WONKA
DANNY THE CHAMPION OF THE WORLD
ESIO TROT
FANTASTIC MR FOX: A Play
GEORGE'S MARVELLOUS MEDICINE
GOING SOLO
JAMES AND THE GIANT PEACH
JAMES AND THE GIANT PEACH: A Play
THE MAGIC FINGER
MATILDA
THE TWITS
THE WITCHES
DIRTY BEASTS (picture book)
THE ENORMOUS CROCODILE (picture book)
THE GIRAFFE AND THE PELLY AND ME (picture book)
REVOLTING RHYMES (picture book)
THE VICAR OF NIBBLESWICKE (for readers of 11+)
THE WONDERFUL STORY OF HENRY SUGAR AND SIX MORE
  (for readers of 11+)

Richard Maher and Sylvia Bond

The
ROALD DAHL
QUIZ BOOK

Illustrated by
Quentin Blake

Scholastic Inc.
New York Toronto London Auckland Sydney

For Richard

Acknowledgments
A Special word of Thanks to my father, John Bond, for his continuous and unstinting support.

To my family and friends and Kevin Gallagher, who rescued my work on the computer.

I would also like to thank Maeve Buichy and the Tyrone Guthrie Centre in Annamakerrig.

ISBN 0-590-02552-X

12 11 10 9 8 7 6 5 4 3 2   8 9/9 0 1 2/0

Printed in the U.S.A.   40
First Scholastic printing, February 1997

Contents

Questions

Charlie and the Chocolate Factory

1   What did Charlie's grandparents do all day?
   a) They ate sweets
   b) They stayed in bed
   c) They played cards

2   Who told Charlie all about the chocolate factory?
   a) Grandpa Joe
   b) Grandpa George
   c) Mr Bucket

3   How do Mr Wonka's sweets come out of the factory?
   a) By lorry
   b) Through the front gate
   c) Through a special trap door in the wall

4   Violet Beauregarde won the third Golden Ticket.
   True or false?

5   What did Mr Bucket do after he lost his job?
   a) He shovelled snow in the streets
   b) He cleaned windows
   c) He cut grass

6 Where did Charlie find the Golden Ticket?
*a) In the first bar of Whipple-Scrumptious
Fudgemallow Delight*
*b) In the second bar of Whipple-Scrumptious
Fudgemallow Delight*

7 What did Mr Willy
Wonka look like?
a) A strange dwarf
b) A tall wizard
c) An extraordinary little man

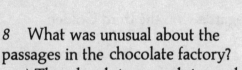

8 What was unusual about the
passages in the chocolate factory?
a) They sloped steeper and steeper downhill
*b) They went round and round in ever-increasing
circles*
*c) They towered layer upon layer like a giant
skyscraper*

9 Where are whangdoodles, hornswogglers and snozzwangers to be found?
   a) In caterpillar country
   b) In Oompa-Loompa land
   c) In eucalyptus land

10 What did Willy Wonka give to Charlie and Grandpa?
   a) Boiled sweets
   b) A mug of warm chocolate
   c) Fizzy lemonade

11 What happened to Violet Beauregarde?
   a) *She turned into a violet*
   b) *She turned into a blueberry*
   c) *She turned into a cauliflower*

12 Why did squirrels start tap-tap-tapping Veruca Salt's head?
   a) *To see if she was a hard nut*
   b) *To see if she was a nutcase*
   c) *To see if she was a bad nut*

13 Which button did Willy Wonka press in the glass lift?
       a) *Up and Out*
       b) *Up and Over*
          c) *Rooftop Garden*

14   How did Charlie and Grandpa Joe come home?
   a) *Through the front door*
   b) *Through the back door*
   c) *Through the roof*

15   When did Charlie get chocolate?
   a) *On Sunday*
   b) *Once a month*
   c) *Once a year*

16   What did Charlie always do in the evenings?
   a) *Watched TV*
   b) *Listened to his grandparents' stories*
   c) *Played cards*

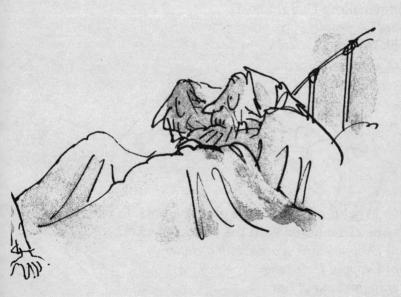

17   How many Golden Tickets were there?
   a) Four
   b) Five
   c) Six

18   What did Veruca Salt's father do?
   a) He owned a peanut factory
   b) He owned a toothbrush factory
   c) He owned a TV station

19   What was Mike Teavee's hobby?
   a) Watching television
   b) Playing cowboys
   c) Playing marbles

20   How much did the Whipple-Scrumptious
Fudgemallow Delight cost?
   a) Five pence
   b) Ten pence
   c) Twenty-five pence

21   What did the four old grandparents do when
Charlie came home with the Golden Ticket?
   a) Dropped their spoons with a clatter
   b) Dropped their soup
   c) Jumped out of bed

22 Who won the first Golden Ticket?
   a) *Martin August*
   b) *Augustus Gloop*
   c) *June Butterfield*

23 Who found the second Golden Ticket?
   a) *Veruca Salt*
   b) *Mike Bunion*
   c) *George Pepper*

24 Why did Mr Wonka go to India?
   a) *To build Prince Pondicherry a chocolate palace*
   b) *To get the Oompa-Loompas*
   c) *To get special spices*

25 Which room in the chocolate factory was 'the nerve centre, the heart of the whole business'?
   a) *The nut room*
   b) *The invention room*
   c) *The chocolate room*

26 What did Willy Wonka promise to pay the Oompa-Loompas for their wages?
   a) Crushed caterpillars
   b) Red beetle soup
   c) Cacao beans and chocolate

27 What kind of chewing gum did Willy Wonka invent?
   a) Five flavour gum
   b) Everlasting flavour gum
   c) Three-course dinner gum

28 Why did Willy Wonka want to give his factory and his sweet-making secrets to a child?
   a) Because sweets are for children
   b) Because grown-ups won't listen
   c) Because of the Oompa-Loompas

29 Who would go to Willy Wonka's chocolate factory with Charlie?
   a) Grandpa Joe
   b) Mr Bucket
   c) Both a) and b)

30 What was Augustus Gloop's hobby?
   a) Eating
   b) Watching TV
   c) Roller-skating

31 Why did Mr Wonka ask his workers to leave?
   a) Because he got machines to do the work
   b) Because of spies who stole his secret recipes
   c) He was moving to Australia

32 Why was Sunday better than the rest of the week for Charlie's family?
   a) It was a day off
   b) Everyone got a second helping

33 What was the prize for finding a Golden Ticket?
   a) A special tour of the chocolate factory
   b) Enough chocolates and sweets to last a lifetime
   c) Both a) and b)

34 What did Charlie
find in the snow?
   a) A Golden Ticket
   b) A bar of chocolate
   c) A fifty-pence piece

35 What was Augustus Gloop doing at the
chocolate river?
   a) He was drinking it by the bucket
   b) He was lapping it like a dog
   c) He was swimming in it

36 What was Mr Wonka's new line in toffees?
   a) Toffee to make your hair grow
   b) Toffee to make your jaws stick together
   c) Toffee to chew like chewing gum

37   What happened to the glass lift when it crashed through the factory roof?
   a) It broke into a million pieces
   b) It shot into space like a rocket
   c) It hovered in the air like a helicopter

38   Mike Teavee was the first person to be sent by television.
   True or false?

39   Fizzy Lifting Drinks make you:
   a) Full with bubbles filled with gas
   b) Shake and frizz with froth
   c) Do a burp

40   What happened to Augustus Gloop?
   a) He was sucked up into a glass pipe
   b) He was swept under the waterfall
   c) He was whipped into a whirlpool

41   Who protected Charlie from the people who tried to buy the Golden Ticket from him?
   a) The policeman
   b) The fat shopkeeper
   c) The tall man

42   What did Professor Foulbody invent?
   a) Foul smell deodorants
   b) A machine to detect Golden Tickets
   c) Sweet-smelling manure

43   How many types of chocolate bar did Mr Wonka invent?
   a) Over fifty
   b) Over one hundred
   c) Over two hundred

44   How many toy guns did Mike Teavee own?
   a) Ten
   b) Twelve
   c) Eighteen

45   What did Grandpa Joe do when he saw the Golden Ticket was real?
   a) He yelled Yippeeeeeeee, leaping out of bed
   b) He did a victory dance in his pyjamas
   c) Both a) and b)

46   How does Willy Wonka mix his chocolate?
   a) By waterfall
   b) By windmill
   c) By whirlpool

47   What did Veruca Salt want?
a) An Oompa-Loompa
b) A good kick in the pants
c) Both a) and b)

48   What was the inventing room like?
a) A witch's kitchen
b) A metal monster
c) A galactic garage

49   Who did Willy Wonka invent the Everlasting Gobstopper for?
a) Children who talked too much
b) Children with big mouths
c) Children with very little pocket money

50   Veruca Salt ended up with all the floor-sweepings, potato peelings, rotten cabages and fish heads.
True or false?

51   What date did Willy Wonka fix for the visit to the chocolate factory?
a) The first of May
b) The first of February
c) The first of July

52   Where did Charlie get the sixpence to buy his second bar of chocolate?
a) He found it
b) Grandpa Joe's secret hoard
c) His dad

53 Who ate Wonka's Whipple-Scrumptious Fudgemallow Delight?
   a) Charlie
   b) Augustus Gloop
   c) Veruca Salt

54 What is different about Mr Wonka's factory?
   a) Nobody comes out or goes in to work
   b) He has secret formulas for sweets
   c) Both a) and b)

55 What was Violet Beauregarde's most treasured possession?
   a) A Golden Ticket
   b) A piece of chewing gum
   c) Her television

56 What was it like inside the chocolate factory?
   a) Like a giant rabbit warren
   b) The rooms were as big as football fields
   c) Both a) and b)

57 What was Willy Wonka's private yacht made of?
   a) Fudgemallow
   b) A candycane
   c) A hollowed-out boiled sweet

58   What made the
Oompa-Loompas tiddly?
   a) Butterscotch and soda
   b) Buttergin and tonic
   c) Both a) and b)

59   What was special about Mr Wonka's ice-
cream?
   a) The taste
   *b) It stayed cold for hours without being in the
   refrigerator*
   c) The colour

60   What did Mr Wonka call Violet Beauregarde?
   a) A jelly bean
   b) A human bean
   c) A has bean

61   What came out of the machine that went
phut-phut-phut phut-phut?
   a) A large green marble
   b) An Everlasting Gobstopper
   c) Both a) and b)

62   What did Charlie long for more than
anything else?
  a) A new bike
  b) Chocolate
  c) Ice-cream

George's Marvellous Medicine

1 Why was George bored to tears?
   a) He had no books
   b) He had no toys
   c) He had no one to play with

2 What did Grandma tell George to eat three times a day?
   a) Cauliflower
   b) Cabbage
   c) Curly kale

3 What shockers did George think up for Grandma?
   a) A firework banger under her chair
   b) A long green snake down her dress
   c) Both a) and b)

4 Why should the flea powder be kept away from the dog's food?
   a) The fleas would eat it
   b) It would make the dog sneeze
   c) It would make the dog explode

5 At what time did George's mother tell him to give Grandma her medicine?
   a) Eleven o'clock
   b) Twelve o'clock
   c) Three o'clock

6   What, according to Grandma, gives you brains?
   a) *Slugs*
   b) *Caterpillars*
   c) *Centipedes*

7   Why did George think Grandma's medicine was not working?
   a) *She was still sick*
   b) *She was just as horrid after taking it as before*
   c) *She was shrinking*

8   Which of these did George *not* find in the bedroom?
   a) *Hair remover*
   b) *Helga's Hairset*
   c) *Pink plaster powder*

9 What did George hope would cure Grandma's sharp tongue?
   a) Hen's gripewater
   b) Hoarse throat horse pills
   c) Pig pills for swine sickness

10 How many doses of the medicine did George give the 'old girl'?
   a) One
   b) Two
   c) Three

11 The hen grew to the size of
   a) A dog
   b) A goat
   c) A horse

12 What was the name of George's pony?
   a) Alma
   b) Grey Shadow
   c) Jack Frost

13 What did George's dad call Grandma?
   a) A grumpy old grouch
   b) A pain in the neck
   c) A wicked old hag

14 What was the trouble about making the second pot of medicine?
   a) George had used up all the ingredients
   b) The pot wasn't big enough
   c) George couldn't remember everything he had put in

15 Why did Grandma drink Marvellous Medicine Number Four?
   a) She thought it was a cup of tea
   b) She wanted to go back to her normal size
   c) She wanted to grow taller

16 Who did Mrs Kranky accuse of having cooked the old girl's goose'?
   a) George
   b) Mr Kranky
   c) Both a) and b)

17 Who did George think was a 'grizzly old grunion'?
   a) The old goat
   b) His grandma
   c) His father

18 How, according to Grandma, should George stop himself growing?
   a) Stand on his head
   b) Drink beetlejuice
   c) Eat less chocolate

19 What do you have to bite before it bites you?
   a) A beetle
   b) A spider
   c) An earwig

20 What cupboard did George avoid when making his medicine?
   a) The poison cupboard
   b) The medicine cupboard
   c) The chemical cupboard

21 If the toothpaste doesn't clean her teeth, then this will paint them as red as roses. What is it?
   a) Scarlet nail varnish
   b) Red hair dye
   c) Red lipstick

22 Where did George go after the laundry-room?
  a) The garage
  b) The kitchen
  c) The shed

23 What animal medicines did George *not* mix in?
  a) Goats' granules
  b) Sheep dip
  c) Chicken powder

24 What colour was the medicine when George boiled it?
  a) Gorgeous gruesome green
  b) Fearsome fiery red
  c) Deep and brilliant blue

25 What did George see when Grandma opened her small wrinkled mouth?
   a) Disgusting pale brown teeth
   b) Two pink little tonsils
   c) Both a) and b)

26 How did George prove that he had made the medicine?
   a) He showed Gran all the empty cans
   b) He gave some to a hen
   c) He let her smell the mixture

27 What was George's dad's first name?
   a) Claus
   b) Billy
   c) Killy

28 What did George add to make the medicine brown?
 a) Dark brown gloss paint
 b) Dark brown shoe polish
 c) A quart of brown beer

29 What happened to George whenever he got a whiff of the mixture?
 a) Firecrackers went off in his skull
 b) Electric prickles ran along the backs of his legs
 c) Both a) and b)

30 What work did George's father do?
 a) He was a salesman
 b) He was a farmer
 c) He was a grocer

31 What did Grandma think was good for you?
 a) A mud bath twice a day
 b) Raw ripe rhubarb
 c) Worms, slugs and beetley bugs

32　How many times a day did Grandma get her medicine?
　　a) Four
　　b) Three
　　c) Twice

33　What did George use to make his medicine in?
　　a) A bucket
　　b) A pressure cooker
　　c) A two-handled saucepan

34　What did George think Gran should have plenty of?
　　a) Brillident – for cleaning false teeth
　　b) Nevermore Ponking Deodorant Spray
　　c) Liquid paraffin

35　Which of these did George get in the kitchen?
　　a) 'Extra hot' chilli sauce
　　b) Cider vinegar
　　c) Both a) and b)

36　What happened after Grandma began to bulge and swell all over?
　　a) She exploded
　　b) She whizzed all around the room like a balloon letting out air
　　c) She developed a puncture

37   What did George's mother do when she saw Grandma sticking up out of the roof?
   a) She goggled and gaped
   b) She looked as if she was going to faint
   c) Both a) and b)

38   Why was George's dad so excited about the medicine?
   a) It had made Grandma grow
   b) He had been trying to breed bigger animals for years
   c) Both a) and b)

39   What was Mr Kranky's great idea?
   a) To build a giant Marvellous Medicine factory
   b) To sell the medicine to old people's homes
   c) To sell the formula to the Government

40   What happened to the chicken with Marvellous Medicine Number Two?
   a) All its feathers fell out
   b) Its legs grew like stilts
   c) Only the body grew; the head and legs were titchy

41   What did George *not* add to Marvellous Medicine Number Four?
   a) Half a pint of engine oil
   b) Anti-freeze
   c) Grease

42   How many doses of the Marvellous Medicine were in the cup?
   a) Twenty
   b) Fifty
   c) Sixty

43   Which two of the following did George forget to add to Marvellous Medicine Number Two?
  a) Flea powder
  b) Vanishing cream
  c) Shoe polish

44   What happened to Grandma when she drank Marvellous Medicine Number Four?
  a) She disappeared
  b) She blew up
  c) She burst her boiler

45   What did George almost forget in Marvellous Medicine Number Two?
  a) A quart of brown gloss paint
  b) Shaving soap
  c) Helga's Hairset

46 Why did George throw in Golden Gloss Hair Shampoo?
  a) *To wash Grandma's tummy nice and clean*
  b) *To put a shine on Grandma*
  c) *To lighten Grandma's hair colour*

47 What did Grandma's small puckered-up mouth look like?
  a) *A buttonhole*
  b) *A fish in a bowl*
  c) *A dog's bottom*

48 What was Grandma's smile like?
  a) *A thin icy smile*
  b) *Like a snake before it bites*
  c) *Both a) and b)*

49 When did Grandma stop growing?
  a) *When she reached the ceiling*
  b) *When she reached the bedroom*
  c) *When she reached the roof*

50   How did Grandma get out of the house?
   a) She wriggled out like a snake
   b) She climbed out
   c) She was lifted out by a crane

51   What effect did Marvellous Medicine Number Three have on the cockerel?
   a) Its beak grew five feet
   b) Its neck grew six feet
   c) Its head grew as big as the moon

52   Where did George's Grandma spend all day?
   a) Sitting by the fire
   b) Sitting by the window
   c) In bed

53   What effect did Marvellous Medicine Number
Four have on the chicken?
   a) Its wings grew as big as an albatross
   b) It shrank to the size of a new-hatched chick
   *c) It ran around in circles and then jumped over the
   house*

54   What, according to Grandma, was wrong with
George?
   a) He was growing too fast
   b) He was disobedient
   c) He ate too much

55   What secrets did Grandma claim she had?
   a) Secret potions
   b) Magic powers
   c) Both a) and b)

56   What rule did George apply to making his medicine?
   a) Everything that would make Grandma better went into it
   b) Everything gooey would go into it
   c) Everything he saw would go into it

57   What did George mix into the medicine to give Grandma a treat?
   a) A bottle of gin
   b) A bottle of whisky
   c) A bottle of vodka

58   Where did Grandma sleep when she was too big to fit in the house?
   a) In the field among the haystacks
   b) In the hay-barn with the mice and rats
   c) In a huge articulated truck

59 Who wanted Grandma to drink Marvellous Medicine Number Four?
  a) George
  b) Mrs Kranky
  c) Mr Kranky

60 When was Grandma mean to George?
  a) All the time
  b) In the morning
  c) When he was alone with her

Fantastic Mr Fox

1 How did Mr Fox get food every day for his family?

   a) He went to the supermarket
   b) He raided the butcher's shop
   c) He raided the three farms

2 What were the names of the three farmers?

   a) Woggis, Dunce and Lean
   b) Moggis, Munce and Mean
   c) Boggis, Bunce and Bean

3 How many small foxes did Mr and Mrs Fox have?

   a) Two
   b) Three
   c) Four

4 How did the farmers try to catch the fox?

   a) They set a trap
   b) They hid with their guns and tried to shoot him
   c) They left their guard dogs out

5   What dirty habit did Bean have?
   a) He picked his nose
   b) He spat
   c) Both a) and b)

6   What was different about the wind the night
Mr Fox was shot?
   a) It was blowing away from the farmers
   b) There was no wind at all
   c) It was a very stormy night

7   Bean's ears were full of dead flies, muck, wax
and bits of chewing-gum.
   True or false?

8   What were the murderous brutal-looking
monsters that Bunce and Bean brought to get the
fox family out of their tunnel?
   a) Big black vicious-looking dogs
   b) Huge robots with shovels for hands
   *c) Two enormous caterpillar tractors with mechanical
   diggers on their front ends*

9   Boggis, Bunce and Bean were:
   a) Rich
   b) Nasty and mean
   c) Both a) and b)

10   Is it farmer Bunce or farmer Bean who has fumes of apple cider hanging about him like poisonous gasses?

11   What did Bean want to do with Fox when he had killed him?
   a) String him up over his front porch
   b) Make a fox rug for in front of the fireplace
   c) Sell the pelt to a fox-fur shop

12   How did Boggis, Bunce and Bean arrange to stay on the hill until the foxes were forced up by hunger?
   a) They took turns on watch
   b) They sent messages down to their farms for tents, sleeping-bags and food
   c) They lit a fire to keep warm

13   How did the farmers make sure that the foxes didn't escape from their den in the dark?
   a) They sat right at the edge of the tunnel with their guns pointed at it
   b) They blocked off the entrance with a huge rock
   c) They switched on the powerful headlamps of the two tractors and shone them on the hole all night

14   Who gave the foxes a fright in the tunnel?
   a) Badger
   b) Weasel
   c) Rabbit

15   What was Bunce's Mighty Storehouse like?
   a) It was a paradise for hungry animals
   b) It was a total mess
   c) It was empty

16   Why did the smallest of the foxes want to bring carrots from Bunce's Mighty Storehouse?
   a) Because he liked them
   b) Because they are good for your eyes
   c) Because rabbits don't eat meat

17   What do badgers use cider for?
   a) For medicine
   b) For steeping fruit in
   c) For refreshing sore paws after a long dig

18   What do Mr Fox and Badger think of Rat?
   a) He has bad manners
   b) He drinks too much
   c) Both a) and b)

19   Why was it important to take just a few ducks and geese from Bunce's Mighty Storehouse?
  a) Because they needed only a few
  b) So that Bunce wouldn't notice
  c) Because they could carry only a few

20   Boggis ate the same thing for breakfast, lunch and supper. It was:
  a) Orange juice, porridge and toast
  b) Three boiled chickens with dumplings
  c) Ten sausages with bacon and one dozen eggs

21   How did Mr Fox avoid being caught by the farmers?
  a) He went to a different farm every night
  b) He kept the wind in his face, so he could sniff the smells of the men on the wind and go another way
  c) He was just plain lucky!

22   Which farmer gave off a filthy stink of rotten chicken-skins?
  a) Boggis
  b) Bunce
  c) Bean

23   Was Mr Fox:
  a) Killed
  b) Only tail-less
  c) Badly wounded

24   Mr Fox knew that the farmers were still at the den's entrance because he could smell Bean.
   True or false?

25   Which fox was weakest from lack of food and water?
   a) Mr Fox
   b) Mrs Fox
   c) The Smallest Fox

26   Why did Mr Fox not tell the small foxes where the new tunnel was going?
   a) He wasn't sure himself
   b) He was afraid they would get excited and make a noise
   c) He was afraid they would be very disappointed if they failed to get there

27   Why did Mr Fox and his children smile when Badger was so cross?
   a) Because they were laughing at him
   b) Because Badger had been digging in circles for three days
   c) Because the foxes shared a secret

28   How did the two Small Foxes carry all the ducks, geese, hams, bacon and carrots back to their mother?
   a) They were extraordinarily strong
   b) They borrowed two push-carts from Bunce
   c) They took them along a few at a time

29 What was different about Bean's cellar?
  a) It was made of wood
  b) It had barbed wire around it
  c) It was made of bricks

30 What kind of fellow was Rat?
  a) He was a gentle old rat
  b) He was very shy
  c) He was a shrieking, fighting, angry rat

31 How were the animals nearly caught in Bean's cellar?
  a) The rat got drunk and smashed a bottle
  b) They got stuck in the hole on the way out
  c) Mabel came down to the cellar to get Bean's supply of cider

32 What happened in the middle of Mr Fox's speech at the feast?
  a) He kept belching
  b) He forgot what he had been going to say
  c) The mechanical digger finally broke into the tunnel

33   What part of the fox was Mabel told she could have as a souvenir when she heard the tail had been shot to pieces?
  a) *The whole body to drape around her neck*
  b) *The head*
  c) *A foot for good luck*

34   What did Badger think of the raid on the farmers' storehouses?
  a) *He thought it might be stealing*
  b) *He thought it was great fun*
  c) *He thought Fox was Fantastic*

35   Boggis, Bunce and Bean had dug a hole so big you could:
  a) *Launch a rocket from it*
  b) *Put a house into it*
  c) *Make a swimming-pool out of it*

36   Bunce was:
  a) *So short his chin was under water in the shallow end of any swimming-pool in the world*
  b) *So heavy he had to travel around on an electric tricycle*
  c) *So bad-tempered that no one would work for him*

37   Where were the three farmers hiding the night Mr Fox was shot?
  a) *On Bean's farm*
  b) *On Bunce's farm*
  c) *Outside Mr Fox's den*

38   How many of these did Boggis, Bunce and
Bean say about Fox?
  'Dang and blast that lousy beast!'
  'I'd like to rip his guts out!'
  'He must be killed!'
  a) One of them
  b) Two of them
  c) All three of them

39   What did the farmers decide to do when they
had missed Mr Fox with their guns?
  a) Dig him out
  b) Send for the hunting dogs
  c) Both a) and b)

40   How did the Fox family escape when the
shovels came through the roof of their den?
  a) By digging deeper
  b) By hiding down another tunnel
  c) They didn't escape; they were trapped!

41   What was Bean's plan after the diggers had
failed to reach the foxes?
  a) To send Bunce down the hole after Fox
  b) To starve the foxes out
  c) Both a) and b)

42 Where did Mr Fox's first new tunnel take them to?

    a) Boggis's Chicken House Number One
    b) The apple orchard
    c) Right into the barrel of a gun!

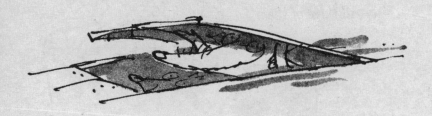

43 What did Mr Fox take from Boggis's Chicken House Number One?

    a) Six juicy chickens
    b) Three dozen eggs
    c) Three of the plumpest hens

44 What did Fox say when Badger asked him about his tail?

    a) 'It's a painful subject'
    b) 'Those foul farmers shot it off'
    c) 'I caught it in the door of Chicken House Number One'

45 What was Bean's cider like?

    a) Melted gold
    b) Drinking sunbeams and rainbows
    c) Both a) and b)

46   Mabel could smell rats in the cellar. What was she told to do about it?
   a) Set traps
   b) Send the cats down
   c) Poison them

47   Bean never ate any food at all.
   True or false?

48   How long did it take the foxes to tunnel deep enough to be away from the terrible sounds of the huge shovels?
   a) Ten minutes
   b) Twenty minutes
   c) One hour

49   What did Mrs Fox think when she saw the three plump hens?
   a) That she was dreaming
   b) That Mr Fox was a Fantastic Fox
   c) Both a) and b)

50   Why was Badger furious with Mr Fox?
   a) Because Mr Fox had dug into Badger's tunnel
   b) Because it was all Mr Fox's fault that they were starving
   c) Because Mr Fox had stood on Badger's tail

51   Who made up the song about having 'Some cider inside her inside'?
  a) Badger
  b) Fox
  c) Both a) and b)

52   Bunce was:
  a) A potato farmer
  b) A cabbage farmer
  c) A duck and goose farmer

53   What difference did Badger make to digging the new tunnel?
  a) He held them up because he was so fat
  b) He was a great digger and the tunnel moved forward at a terrific pace
  c) He kept going in the wrong direction

54   How may of the following names did Rat call Mr Fox and Badger?
  Thieves
  Robbers
  Bandits
  Burglars
  a) Two of them
  b) All of them
  c) None of them

55   What was Mr Fox's plan for the animals?
   *a) To make an underground village, with houses for
   each family*
   *b) To make a huge cave for everyone to live in all
   together*
   *c) To move to another hill, far away from Boggis
   and Bunce and Bean*

Esio Trot

1 Esio Trot was:
   a) A tortoise
   b) A turtle
   c) An armadillo

2 Mr Hoppy loved:
   a) A tortoise
   b) His dog
   c) His flowers

3 What did Mr Hoppy feel when he looked at Mrs Silver?
   a) That she was sweet, gentle and kind
   b) That she would never love him
   c) Both a) and b)

4 Where did Mr Hoppy learn the secret of making things grow?
   a) In North Africa
   b) In Ballydehob
   c) In Iceland

5 How many tortoises did Mr Hoppy buy?
   a) One hundred and forty
   b) One hundred and sixty
   c) Fifty-six

6 How did Mrs Silver discover that her tortoise, Alfie, had grown?
   a) He couldn't fit into her slipper any more
   b) He couldn't fit into his house any more
   c) He was so heavy he could hardly move

7   Who did Mrs Silver think was the 'cleverest man alive'?
   a) *The bedouin tribesman who knew tortoise language*
   b) *Esio Trot*
   c) *Mr Hoppy*

8   Mr Hoppy lived in:
   a) *A tall concrete building*
   b) *A country cottage*
   c) *A large mansion*

9   Why did Mr Hoppy want to become a tortoise?
   a) *Because he had not got enough money to buy food*
   b) *Because he wanted to be someone's pet*
   c) *Because he wanted Mrs Silver to stroke his shell and whisper nice things to him*

10   What did Mrs Silver want for Alfie?
   a) She wanted him to grow bigger
   b) She wanted a little jacket to keep him warm
   c) She wanted another tortoise so he wouldn't feel lonely

11   Why are words written backwards in tortoise language?
   a) Because they are backward creatures
   b) Because they walk backwards
   c) Because they come from China

12   What did Mr Hoppy buy to make Alfie look bigger?
   a) Special 'Grow Quick' food
   b) At least one hundred tortoises of different weights and sizes
   c) A large magnifying glass

13   What did the tortoises eat?
   a) *Bacon, lettuce and tomato*
   b) *Cream cheese and crackers*
   c) *Cabbage leaves and water*

14   Mrs Silver went out every day:
   a) *To work in a sweet-shop*
   b) *To go to keep-fit classes*
   c) *To visit the pet shop*

15   Why did Tortoise Number 2 eat so much?
   a) *Because he was bigger than Alfie and needed more food*
   b) *Because the other tortoises weren't there to take food from him*
   c) *Because the lovely, tender, juicy lettuce leaves Mrs Silver fed him were so much nicer than old cabbage leaves*

16   How long did Mr Hoppy wait before he changed tortoises again?
   a) *Five days*
   b) *Seven days*
   c) *Ten days*

17   How big had 'Alfie' grown in seven weeks?
   a) He was now twenty ounces
   b) He was twenty-five ounces
   c) He was twenty-seven ounces

18   Why was Mrs Silver crying when 'Alfie' had
grown small enough to fit into his little house again?
   a) Because she realized it wasn't Alfie
   b) Because she was so happy
   c) Because his tail still wouldn't fit in

19   Mr Hoppy was:
   a) A very happy man
   b) A very cranky man
   c) A very lonely man

20   What prevented 'Alfie' from toppling over
the edge of the balcony?
   a) An electric wire fence
   b) Planks all around the sides
   c) Lots of big, heavy flower-pots

21   Who was Mr Hoppy's secret love?
   a) Mrs Silver
   b) Mrs Golden
   c) Mrs Sunshine

22 Where did 'Alfie' sleep at night?
  a) On Mrs Silver's pillow
  b) In a little wicker basket
  c) In a little house on the balcony

23 How was Mrs Silver to work the magic formula on Alfie?
  a) She was to put the words under the straw in his little house
  b) She was to whisper them in his ear three times a day
  c) She was to walk around Alfie three times, chanting the words

24 What had Mr Hoppy worked at before he retired?
  a) He had been an engineer
  b) He had been a mechanic
  c) He had been a carpenter

25 Mr Hoppy made something to lift a tortoise from Mrs Silver's balcony. Was it:
a) A little cage on a pulley like a lift
b) A green net with a lettuce leaf on it that could be pulled up
c) Two metal claws attached to a long pole with wires to open and close the claws

26 How did Mr Hoppy feel when Mrs Silver was so pleased with the secret formula?
a) He was delighted
b) He was over the moon with happiness
c) He was quivering all over with excitement

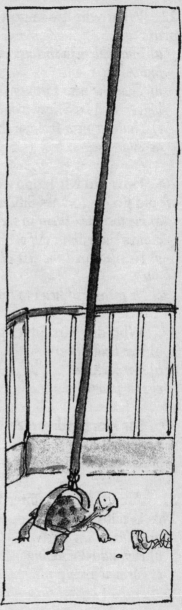

27   What was the important thing in Mr Hoppy's plan?

a) That the new tortoise should have a spot exactly like Alfie

b) That the new tortoise should be only a tiny bit bigger so Mrs Silver wouldn't notice

c) That the new tortoise should look just as gorgeous as Alfie

28   How did Mr Hoppy choose which tortoise would go on to Mrs Silver's balcony?

a) He weighed them to see they were exactly two ounces more than Alfie

b) He measured the size of the shell to get a wider one

c) He measured head to tail to get a longer one

29   Who did Mrs Silver give all her love to?

a) Her teddy bear

b) Her tortoise

c) Her poodle

30   Mr Hoppy dreamed of being a hero who saves Mrs Silver.

True or false?

31   Alfie slept all winter without food or water. This is called:

a) Hibernating

b) Rip-Van-Winkling

c) Forty-winking

32   What did Alfie weigh?
   a) *Ten ounces – like an orange*
   b) *Thirteen ounces – like a grapefruit*
   c) *Twenty ounces – like a melon*

33   Who told Mr Hoppy the secret formula for
making things grow?
   a) *A leprechaun*
   b) *A bedouin tribesman*
   c) *An eskimo*

34   What did Mrs Silver promise if Mr Hoppy
told her the secret formula?
   a) *She would be his slave for life*
   b) *She would be his best friend for life*
   c) *She would bake him a cake every Saturday for the
   rest of his life*

35   What was the one thing that had to match in
all the tortoises?
   a) *The colour of their shell*
   b) *The shape of their heads*
   c) *Their toenails*

36   How did Mr Hoppy solve the problem of the
tortoise-house-that-was-too-small?
   a) *He made the tortoise grow smaller*
   b) *He cut the door to enlarge it*
   c) *He made a new tortoise house*

37   How did Mr Hoppy make the tortoise grow smaller?
   a) He fed it on only water and one leaf for a week
   b) He wrote out tortoise language for Mrs Silver to make him smaller
   c) He gave him two shrinking pills

38   How did Mr Hoppy *really* make the tortoise grow smaller?
   a) He simply put a smaller tortoise on the balcony
   b) He shaved the edge of the tortoise house and repainted it
   c) He put Alfie on a diet to slim him down

39   How did Mr Hoppy prevent the tortoise from getting titchy small all over again?
   a) Mrs Silver read the shrinking formula only twice
   b) He told Mrs Silver to give Alfie plenty of protein
   c) He built a tortoise body-building gym

40 Why did Mr Hoppy jump over the tortoises like a ballet dancer and fly down the stairs two at a time?

    a) Because he was very much in love with Mrs Silver
    b) Because Mrs Silver's kitchen was flooded
    c) Because his balcony was on fire

41 What did Mr Hoppy need to do when Mrs Silver agreed to marry him?

    a) To buy two tickets to Bermuda for a honeymoon
    b) To buy a new house with a large garden for all the tortoises
    c) To take all the other tortoises back to the pet shop and clean up his flat

42   What happened to little Alfie?
   a) *It took him thirty years to grow too big to fit into the little house*
   b) *He still lives with the little girl who bought him*
   c) *Both a) and b)*

The Giraffe and the Pelly and Me

1   What does the word Grubber mean?
   a) It is an old word for a sweet-shop
   b) It is a name for someone who is very dirty
   c) It is a name for someone who eats too quickly

2   How did the new owners clear out The Grubber?
   a) They had workmen in who wore blue overalls
   b) They got a skip and put all the rubbish in it
   c) They threw everying out of the second-floor window

3   What was unusual about the new door of The Grubber?
   a) It was twice as high as the last one
   b) It was red instead of brown
   c) It was as wide as a barn door

4   What was so special about this window-cleaning company?
   a) They didn't ever use ladders
   b) They were all animals
   c) Both a) and b)

5   What was Pelly's beak known as?
  a) *The Cavernous Carryall Superholder*
  b) *The Pelican's Patented Beak*
  c) *The Basin and Bucket Beak*

6   What is so scrumptious-galumptious, so flavory-savory, so sweet to eat, for the Monkey?
  a) *Bunches of bananas*
  b) *Fresh walnuts*
  c) *Glorious salmon*

7   What was the name of the Duke's mansion?
  a) *Hampshire House*
  b) *Huckleberry House*
  c) *Hiccup House*

8   What was the gardener trying to do on the ladder?
  a) *To clean the windows*
  b) *To reach the biggest juicy cherries at the top of the tree*
  c) *To shape the hedge into a hedgehog*

9   Name the animal who did each job in the Ladderless-Window-Cleaning Company.
  a) *The ladder*
  b) *The bucket*
  c) *The window-cleaner*

10   What did the Pelly do to stop the thief
causing trouble inside his beak?
   a) He filled his beak with water so the thief had to
   keep swimming
   b) He shook his head rapidly from side to side to
   rattle his bones
   c) He flew around upside-down until the thief was
   dizzy

11   What was the name of the famous opera
singer who burst into song about the missing
diamonds?
   a) Helga
   b) Higginsbottom
   c) Henrietta

12   The Giraffe ate only:
   a) Green and purple French grapes
   b) The delicate leaves of the ju-jubee tree
   c) The pink and purple flowers of the tinkle-tinkle
   tree

13   What happened when the Duke got excited?
   a) His face went red and purple
   b) His eyes popped out like poppers
   c) His moustaches jumped about as though he had a
   squirrel on his face

14   The queer old empty wooden house stands:
   a) Dwarfed in the middle of skyscrapers
   b) All by itself on the side of the road
   c) In a row of old, broken-down houses

15   The notice on the house said:
   a) FOR SALE, *and after,* SOLD
   b) FOR SALE, *and after,* SOLED
   c) FOR SAIL, *and after,* SOLED

16   What was the first thing that came sailing out
of the window of The Grubber?
   a) An enormous bathtub
   b) A white procelain lavatory pan
   c) A kitchen sink

17   The little boy wished he could own a sweet-
shop filled with:
   a) Sugar Snorters and Butter Gumballs
   b) Sherbert Suckers and Russian Toffee
   c) All of these and more

18   Who stared with big round dark eyes from
the top floor of The Grubber?
   a) The Giraffe
   b) The Pelly
   c) The Monkey

19   Which of the following had the Pelly never
heard of?
   a) A fish-finger
   b) A fish-monger
   c) A fish-cake

20   What was magical and unbelievable about the Pelly's beak?
  a) It could bend and go down inside the back of his neck
  b) It was like a metal tape-measure
  c) Both a) and b)

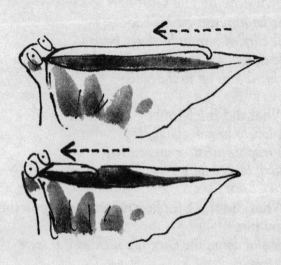

21   What was the little boy's name?
  a) Billy
  b) Johnny
  c) Jimmy

22   How did the Duke know the Giraffe was a Geraneous Giraffe and ate only the flowers of the tinkle-tinkle tree?
  a) He was an expert on the animals of Africa
  b) The Monkey told him
  c) The Duke's friend had one in a private zoo

23 Why did Billy and the Pelly pick the cherries?
  a) To put the Duke in good humour
  b) Because they were starving
  c) To help the gardener

24 How did the Pelly carry the boy up to the house?
  a) He let him ride on his back
  b) He carried him in his huge beak
  c) He caught his shoulders with his soft webbed feet and lifted him up to the house

25 What did the Monkey look like?
  a) A lovely brown cuddly toy
  b) A trapeze artist or an acrobat
  c) Furry bits of wire

26 What did the Monkey do the first time the boy saw him?
  a) He slid down the Giraffe's neck as if it were banisters
  b) He did a jiggly dance and sang a song
  c) He started cleaning all of the windows of the shop

27   The animals:
  a) *Invited the boy to tea*
  b) *Were starving, famished and perishing with hunger*
  c) *Were growing a vegetable garden*

28   Who owned the white Rolls-Royce driven by a chauffeur?
  a) *The Duke of Hampshire*
  b) *The Duke of Buckingham*
  c) *The Duchess of Dorset*

29   What did the Monkey say when he saw all the windows in the mansion?
  a) *'We'll never be able to do all of those'*
  b) *'They'll keep us going for ever'*
  c) *'Let's get started!'*

30   What did the Duke think the Pelly was doing with the cherries?
  a) *Making cherry juice*
  b) *Making cherry jam*
  c) *Stealing them*

31   What was more wonderful than the Pelican's Patented Beak?
  a) *The Giraffe's Magical Neck*
  b) *The Monkey's Balancing Tricks*
  c) *The Window-Cleaning Formula*

32   Why did the animals all freeze against the wall of the Duke's house?
   a) *The Monkey began to lose balance*
   b) *They saw a thief in one of the rooms*
   c) *Giraffe's neck became very stiff*

33   What secret weapon did the Duke have inside his walking stick?
   a) *A mini-machine gun*
   b) *A revolving rifle*
   c) *A super-sharp sword*

34   What made the Duke's eyes nearly pop out of their sockets?
   a) *The Giraffe*
   b) *Billy in the Pelican's beak*
   c) *The skinny Monkey*

35   What was the old Duke doing when the animals arrived?
   a) *He was shouting at the gardener*
   b) *He was playing golf*
   c) *He was swimming in a giant swimming-pool shaped like a harp*

36   What part does the Pelican play in the Ladderless Window-Cleaning Company?
   a) *His beak is the bucket that holds the water*
   b) *He dries the windows with his mop of tail feathers*
   c) *He flies around checking that all the windows are closed*

37   The Pelican was so hungry he could eat:
a) A rotten cod
b) A stale sardine
c) Both a) and b)

38   How many windows are in the Duke's house?
a) Two hundred and fifty
b) Five hundred and sixty-six
c) Six hundred and seventy-seven

39   What was the extra job the Duke asked the window-cleaners to do?
a) To paint all the window frames
b) To clean the chimneys
c) To pick his apples in the autumn

40   Why did the Duke tell them not to bother with the two top floors?
a) Nobody ever used them anyway
b) They were too high up to notice they were dirty
c) He thought the Giraffe couldn't reach

41   Why was the Duke delighted with the clean windows?
a) He thought the animals had done the best job ever
b) He hadn't seen out of his windows for forty years
c) He had wanted to look in through the windows from the garden

42   What made the Pelly leap twenty feet into the air?
   a) He stood on a thorn
   b) A revolver went off inside his beak
   c) The Duke spiked him with his sword

43   What was the name of the thief?
   a) The Slithery Snake
   b) The Rotten Rattler
   c) The Cobra

44   Monkey had his delicious walnuts, Pelly had scrumptious salmon, what was Billy's wish?
   a) To own a large sparkling diamond
   b) To go on a Round-the-World trip
   c) To own The Grubber

45   When The Grubber was all restored and stocked up, which sweets came from Willy Wonka's factory itself?
   a) The Rainbow Drops which let you spit in seven different colours
   b) The Stickjaw for talkative parents
   c) The Mint Ju-jubees, that gave the boy next door green teeth for a month

46   What sweets did the Giraffe get from Billy?
*a) Glumptious Globgobblers with all the juices of
Arabia*
b) Sherbert Slurpers to slurp down his long gullet
*c) Tongue Rakers that raked your tongue with
fabulous flavours*

47   What was Monkey's present?
*a) Giant Whangdoodles from Australia with
strawberries inside*
b) Frothblowers and Spitsizzlers from Africa
c) Devil's Drenchers that set your breath on fire

48   Who sings the farewell song about the Giraffe
and the Pelly and Me?
a) The Duke
b) The Monkey
c) Billy

49   Besides window-cleaning and apple-picking,
what else could the Pelly do for the Duke?
*a) He could check that there were no burglars in the
house*
b) He could catch some salmon for him
c) He could give the Duke a ride in his beak

50   What was the message the chauffeur carried?
a) An invitation to tea
b) A request to visit the zoo
c) An invitation to clean windows

51   How did Billy and the Pelly calm the Duke
down?
   a) They gave him a drink of brandy
   b) They gave him the juicy cherries
   c) They sang a lullaby

52   Billy was part of the team. What was his job?
   a) He was the Business Manager
   b) He was chief Bucket-Holder
   c) He changed the water

53   How was the bullet-hole in the Pelly's beak
repaired?
   a) The chauffeur patched it the same way he patched
   the tyre of the Rolls-Royce
   b) They filled the hole with chewing-gum, like they
   repaired old airplanes
   c) They used special plastic glue to keep it waterproof

54   How did the Duke reward the animals for
saving millions-worth of diamonds?
   a) He gave them thousands of pounds
   b) He gave them a home on his Estate with every
   comfort they desired
   c) He promised to take them back to Africa

55   Which gift of special sweets did Billy give to the Duke?
   a) Liplickers from the land of the Midnight Sun
   b) Scarlet Scorchdroppers from Iceland, guaranteed to keep you warm
   c) Electric Fizzcocklers to make his moustaches stand out on end

56   What never ends when it's full of your friends?
   a) Your own gang
   b) Your birthday party
   c) A book

57   Who came to the Duke's rescue?
   a) Pelly with his Marvellous Beak
   b) Giraffe with his Magical Neck
   c) Monkey with his Tremendous Talent

Matilda

1   What was Matilda's surname?
   a) Wormwood
   b) Woodworm
   c) Woodbrook

2   Which book by Charles Dickens did Matilda
first read?
   a) Oliver Twist
   b) A Christmas Carol
   c) Great Expectations

3   What did Mr Wormwood work as?
   a) A car dealer
   b) A zoo keeper
   c) A clown

4   Why did Mr Wormwood call Matilda a cheat?
   a) Because she cheated at Monopoly
   b) Because she told lies
   c) Because she was good at sums

5 What was the name of the Headmistress at Matilda's school?
   a) Miss Bulldoze
   b) Miss Trunchbull
   c) Miss Caterpillar

6 Who was Matilda's favourite teacher?
   a) Mr Marmalade
   b) Mrs Mutton
   c) Miss Honey

7 What hairstyle did Miss Trunchbull like the least on little girls?
   a) Ribbons
   b) Pigtails
   c) Bun

8 What first amazed Miss Honey about Matilda?
   a) Her mathematical ability
   b) Her musical ability
   c) Her reading ability

9 What is Miss Trunchbull's idea of the perfect school?
   a) Her school
   b) One with no children in it

10 What is Miss Trunchbull's first name?
   a) Primrose
   b) Maggie
   c) Agatha

11 Who was the librarian who helped Matilda with her reading?

   a) Mrs Phearson
   b) Mrs Phelps
   c) Mrs Pheasant

12 What did Matilda use to stick her father's hat to his head?

   a) Sellotape
   b) Gum
   c) Superglue

13 What did Matilda compose for Miss Honey on her first day at school?

   a) A story
   b) A song
   c) A limerick

14 Which did Miss Trunchbull think is worse: *A bad girl or a bad boy?*

15 Why did Miss Honey visit Matilda's parents?
 a) To tell them Matilda was expelled
 b) To complain about Matilda
 c) To tell them Matilda was a brilliant child

16 What did Miss Trunchbull accuse Matilda of doing on her first day at school?
 a) Stealing a pencil
 b) Chewing gum
 c) Putting a stinkbomb under her desk

17 Who put itching-powder in the Trunchbull's knickers?
 a) Matilda
 b) Hortensia
 c) Lavender

18 For what did Amanda Thripp get into trouble?
 a) Eating sweets
 b) Her hairstyle

19 Which of the following did Miss Trunchbull call Bruce Bogtrotter?
 a) A blackhead
 b) A foul carbuncle
 c) A poisonous pustule
 d) A miserable little gumboil

20 How does Miss Honey teach pupils to spell
hard words?
   a) She writes them on the blackboard
   b) She makes up a song about them
   c) She repeats them

21 Who, according to Miss Trunchbull, should
be kept out of sight in boxes like hairpins and
buttons?
   a) Matilda
   b) Small people

22 Who did Miss Trunchbull accuse of putting
the newt in her glass of water?
   a) Hortensia
   b) Matilda

23 Where did Miss Honey live?
   a) In her father's house
   b) In a flat
   c) In a tiny cottage

24 What did Matilda's mum do five afternoons a week?
   a) Go bowling
   b) Play bingo
   c) Play bridge

25 What did Matilda put in her dad's hair oil?
   a) Glue
   b) Grow-again hair tonic for bald men
   c) Platinum blonde hair-dye

26 Who thinks that looks are more important than books?
   a) Miss Trunchbull
   b) Mrs Wormwood
   c) Mrs Phelps

27 Why did Julius Rottwinkle get into trouble?
   a) He got all his spellings wrong
   b) He was eating sweets in class

28 Why did Bruce Bogtrotter get into trouble?
   a) He was cheating
   b) He stole Miss Trunchbull's slice of cake

29   What punishment did Miss Trunchbull give
Bruce Bogtrotter?
   a) Put him in The Chokey
   b) Forced him to eat an enormous cake

30   Who put a newt in Miss Trunchbull's jug of
water?
   a) Matilda
   b) Lavender
   c) Bruce Bogtrotter

31   Who did Miss Trunchbull call 'a witless weed,
an ignorant little slug, a stupid glob of glue'?
   a) Rupert
   b) Lavender

32   What did Miss Trunchbull do to Rupert when
he missed his multiplication tables?
   a) She turned him upside down
   b) She lifted him up by the hair

33   What did Miss Trunchbull often think of
inventing?
   a) A spray for getting rid of small children
   b) An electric cane

34   How did Matilda discover that she had an
extraordinary power?
   a) When she got angry
   b) She read about it

35 What was Matilda's first miracle?
 a) *She toppled the glass of water and the newt over Miss Trunchbull*
 b) *She wrote with the chalk*

36 Why did Matilda think Miss Honey was poor?
 a) *She had no money*
 b) *She ate margarine*
 c) *Her cottage was tiny*

37 Who did Miss Trunchbull call 'a festering gumboil, a fleabitten fungus, a bursting blister and a moth-eaten maggot'?
 a) *Miss Honey*
 b) *Matilda*
 c) *Wilfred*

38   What was Matilda's brother called?
a) John
b) Michael
c) Trevor

39   Who did Miss Trunchbull think was a real
pillar of society?
a) Mr Samson
b) Mr Wormwood
c) Mr Rock

40   What was The Chokey?
a) A sweet
b) A chair
c) A lock-up cupboard

41   What was the Golden Syrup Job?
a) When Hortensia poured a tin of Golden Syrup on
the Trunchbull's chair
b) Sweet-talk to sell cars
c) A method of catching bees

42   What did Hortensia do to Ollie Bogwhistle
for sneaking on her?
a) She locked him in The Chokey
b) She knocked his front teeth out
c) She poured Golden Syrup over his head

43   Why did Miss Trunchbull break a plate over
Bruce Bogtrotter's head?
a) Because her cane was missing
b) Because he succeeded in eating the cake

44   What word could Eric Ink not spell?
   a) Write
   b) Difficulty
   c) What

45   What happened to the car Miss Trunchbull
bought from Matilda's dad?
   a) It crashed
   b) A wheel fell off
   c) Its engine fell out

46   Who did Matilda confide in about her special
power?
   a) Her mother
   b) Miss Honey

47   How did Miss Honey test Matilda's special
power?
   a) On a piece of chalk
   b) On a glass of water

48   What was the name of Miss Honey's father?
   a) Martin
   b) Magnus
   c) Simon

49 What was Matilda's third miracle?
  a) She toppled another glass over
  b) She wrote on the board with chalk

50 Where did Matilda's family eat their meals?
  a) In the kitchen
  b) In front of the telly
  c) In the dining-room

51 What was Miss Trunchbull once famous as?
  a) An athlete
  b) A musician
  c) A detective

52 Who is Miss Honey's aunt?
  a) Matilda's mother
  b) Miss Trunchbull

53 Why had Miss Honey no money?
  a) She was badly paid
  b) Miss Trunchbull took all her salary

54 Why, according to Miss Honey, did Matilda's powers disappear?
  a) She was no longer angry
  b) She was now using all her brains in the top form

55   What did Miss Trunchbull do when she saw Matilda's ghostly writing on the blackboard?
   a) She ran away
   b) She fainted
   c) She yelled

56   Why did Matilda's family go abroad?
   a) For a holiday
   b) Because Matilda's dad was wanted by the police

57   How did Miss Trunchbull cheat Miss Honey out of her inheritance?
   a) She forged her father's will
   b) She ran away with the money

58   What was Miss Honey's family home called?
   a) The Red House
   b) The Pines
   c) Trunchbull Hall

59   How did Matilda suspect that Miss Honey's father died?
   a) He killed himself
   b) Miss Trunchbull murdered him

60   Where did Matilda live after her family went to Spain?
   a) With Miss Trunchbull
   b) With Miss Honey
   c) In an orphanage

Answers

Charlie and the Chocolate Factory

1   b) They stayed in bed

2   a) Grandpa Joe

3   c) Through a special trap door in the wall

4   True

5   a) He shovelled snow in the streets

6   b) In the second bar

7   c) An extraordinary little man

8   a) They sloped steeper and steeper downhill

9   b) In Oompa-Loompa land

10   b) A mug of warm chocolate

11   b) She turned into a blueberry

12   c) To see if she was a bad nut

13   a) Up and Out

14   c) Through the roof

15   c) Once a year, on his birthday

16   b) Listened to his grandparents' stories

17   b) Five

18   a) He owned a peanut factory

19   a) Watching television

20   a) Five pence

21   a) Dropped their spoons with a clatter

22   b) Augustus Gloop

23   a) Veruca Salt

24   a) To build Prince Pondicherry a chocolate palace

25   c) The chocolate room

26   c) Cacao beans and chocolate

27   c) Three-course dinner gum

28   b) Because grown-ups won't listen

29   a) Grandpa Joe

30   a) Eating — he was enormously fat

31   b) Because of spies who stole his secret recipes

32   b) Everyone got a second helping

33   c) Both a) and b)

34   c) A fifty-pence piece

35   b) He was lapping it like a dog

36   a) Toffee to make your hair grow

37   c) It hovered in the air like a helicopter

38   True

39   a) It fills you with bubbles made of a special kind of gas

40   a) He was sucked up into a glass pipe

41   b) The fat shopkeeper

42   b) A machine to detect Golden Tickets

43   c) Over two hundred

44   c) Eighteen

45   c) Both a) and b)

46   a) By waterfall

47   c) Both a) and b)

48   a) A witch's kitchen

49   c) Children with very little pocket money

50   True

51   b) The first of February

52   b) Grandpa Joe's secret hoard

53   a) Charlie — it was his birthday present

54   c) Both a) and b)

55   b) A piece of chewing gum — she had been working on it for three months solid

56   c) Both a) and b)

57   c) A hollowed-out boiled sweet

58   c) Both a) and b)

59   b) It stayed cold for hours without being in the refrigerator

60   c) A has bean

61   b) An Everlasting Gobstopper

62   b) Chocolate

George's Marvellous Medicine

1   c) He had no one to play with

2   b) Cabbage

3   c) Both a) and b)

4   c) It will make the dog explode

5   a) Eleven o'clock

6   b) Caterpillars

7   b) She was just as horrid after taking it as before

8   a) Hair remover

9   b) Hoarse throat horse pills

10   b) Two – he gave her a second one in his bedroom

11   c) A horse

12   c) Jack Frost

13   b) A pain in the neck

14   c) George couldn't remember everything he had put in

15   a) She thought it was a cup of tea

16   b) Mr Kranky – he told Gran to drink it

17   b) His grandma

18   c) Eat less choclate

19   c) An earwig

20   b) The medicine cupboard – he had been forbidden to touch it

21   a) Scarlet nail varnish

22   b) The kitchen

23   a) Goats' granules

24   c) Deep and brilliant blue

25   a) Disgusting pale brown teeth

26   b) He gave some to a hen

27   c) Mr Killy Kranky

28   a) Dark brown gloss paint

29   c) Both a) and b)

30   b) He was a farmer

31   c) Worms, slugs and beetley bugs

32   a) Four

33   c) A two-handled saucepan

34   b) Nevermore Ponking Deodorant Spray — guaranteed to keep away unpleasant body smells for a whole day

35   a) 'Extra hot' chilli sauce

36   c) She developed a puncturè

37   c) Both a) and b)

38   b) He had been trying to breed bigger animals for years

39   a) To build a giant Marvellous Medicine factory

40   b) Its legs grew like stilts

41   c) Grease

42   b) Fifty

43   a) and c) He forgot flea powder and shoe polish

44   a) She disappeared — she became smaller and smaller until there was nothing left

45   a) A quart of brown gloss paint

46   a) To wash Grandma's tummy nice and clean

47   c) A dog's bottom

48   c) Both a) and b)

49   c) When she reached the roof

50   c) She was lifted out by a crane

51   b) Its neck grew six feet

52   b) Sitting by the window

53   b) It shrank to the size of a new-hatched chick

54   a) He was growing too fast

55   b) Magic powers

56   c) Everything he saw would go into it

57   a) A bottle of gin — Grandma was very fond of it

58   b) In the hay-barn with the mice and rats

59   c) Mr Kranky

60   c) When he was alone with her

Fantastic Mr Fox

1   c) He raided the farms

2   c) Boggis, Bunce and Bean

3   c) Four

4   b) They hid with their guns
and tried to shoot him

5   a) He picked his nose —
delicately, with a long finger

6   a) It was blowing away from
the farmers

7   True — Bean never washed
and as a result his earholes were
clogged with all kinds of dirt,
which made him deaf

8   c) Two enormous caterpillar
tractors with mechanical diggers
on their front ends

9   c) Both a) and b)

10   It's farmer Bean, who drinks
nothing but cider

11   a) String him up over his
front porch — dead as a dumpling

12   b) They sent messages down
to their farms for tents, sleeping-
bags and food

13   c) They switched on the
powerful headlamps of the two
tractors and shone them on the
hole all night

14   a) Badger

15   a) It was a paradise for
hungry animals

16   c) Because rabbits don't eat
meat

17   a) For medicine

18   c) Both a) and b)

19   b) So that Bunce wouldn't
notice Mr Fox had been there

20   b) Three boiled chickens
with dumplings

21   b) He kept the wind in his
face, so he could sniff the smells
of the men on the wind and go
another way

22   a) Boggis

23   b) Only tail-less — but it hurt!

24   True

25   b) Mrs Fox

26   c) He was afraid they would be very disappointed if they failed to get there

27   c) Because the Foxes shared a secret

28   b) They borrowed two push-carts from Bunce

29   c) It was made of bricks — to keep the cider cool

30   c) He was a shrieking, fighting, angry rat

31   c) Mabel came down to the cellar to get Bean's supply of cider

32   a) He kept belching

33   b) The head

34   a) He thought it might be stealing

35   b) Put a house into it

36   a) So short that his chin would have been under water in the shallow end of any swimming-pool in the world

37   c) Outside Mr Fox's den

38   c) All three of them

39   a) Dig him out — because they were determined to catch him

40   a) By digging deeper

41   c) Both a) and b)

42   a) Boggis's Chicken House Number One

43   c) Three of the plumpest hens

44   a) 'It's a painful subject' — he didn't want to talk about it

45   c) Both a) and b)

46   c) Poison them

47   True

48   One hour

49   c) Both a) and b)

50   b) Because it was all Mr Fox's fault that they were starving

51 c) Both a) and b)

52 c) A duck and goose farmer

53 b) He was a great digger and the tunnel moved forward at a terrific pace

54 b) All of them

55 a) To make an underground village, with houses for each family

Esio Trot

1   a) A tortoise – try to spell Esio Trot backwards!

2   c) His flowers – he grew them on his balcony

3   a) That she was sweet, gentle and kind – and his heart ached with love

4   a) In North Africa

5   a) One hundred and forty

6   b) He couldn't fit into his house any more

7   c) Mr Hoppy

8   a) A tall concrete building – in a small flat, high up

9   c) Because he wanted Mrs Silver to stroke his shell and whisper nice things to him

10   a) She wanted him to grow bigger – she thought he must feel miserable being so titchy

11   a) Because they are backward creatures – and therefore they can understand only words that are written backwards

12   b) At least one hundred tortoises of different weights and sizes

13   c) Cabbage leaves and water

14   a) To work in a sweet-shop – she was there from noon till five every day

15   c) Because the lovely, tender juicy lettuce leaves Mrs Silver fed him were so much nicer than old cabbage leaves

16   b) Seven days – then he put a heavier tortoise on Mrs Silver's balcony

17   c) He was twenty-seven ounces

18   b) Because she was so happy

19   c) A very lonely man

20   b) Planks all around the side — these meant Alfie could walk about quite safely

21   a) Mrs Silver — but he never told her because he was too shy

22   c) In a little house on the balcony

23   b) She was to whisper them in his ear three times a day — morning, noon and night

24   b) He had been a mechanic

25   c) Two metal claws attached to a long pole with wires to open and close the claws

26   c) He was quivering all over with excitement

27   b) That the new tortoise should be only a tiny bit bigger so Mrs Silver wouldn't notice

28   a) He weighed them to see they were exactly two ounces more than Alfie

29   b) Her tortoise

30   True

31   a) Hibernating

32   b) Thirteen ounces — like a grapefruit

33   b) A bedouin tribesman — from North Africa

34   a) She would be his slave for life

35   a) The colour of their shell

36   a) He made the tortoise grow smaller — Mr Hoppy told Mrs Silver that it would be a shame to go cutting up such a pretty little house; it would be much easier to make Alfie a tiny bit smaller

37   b) He wrote out tortoise language for Mrs Silver to make him grow smaller

38   a) He simply put a smaller tortoise on the balcony

39   a) Mrs Silver read the shrinking formula only twice

40   a) Because he was very much in love with Mrs Silver

41   c) To take all the other tortoises back to the pet shop and clean up his flat

42   c) Both a) and b)

The Giraffe and the Pelly and Me

1 a) It is an old word for a sweet-shop

2 c) They threw everything out of the second-floor window

3 a) It was twice as high as the last one

4 c) Both a) and b)

5 b) The Pelican's Patented Beak

6 b) Fresh walnuts

7 a) Hampshire House

8 b) To reach the biggest juicy cherries at the top of the tree

9 a) The Giraffe was the ladder, with his Magical Neck
   b) The Pelly's Patented Beak held the water
   c) The Monkey cleaned the windows

10 b) He shook his head rapidly from side to side to rattle his bones

11 c) Her name was Henrietta

12 c) The pink and purple flowers of the tinkle-tinkle tree

13 c) His moustaches jumped about as though he had a squirrel on his face

14 b) All by itself on the side of the road

15 c) FOR SAIL, and after, SOLED

16 a) An enormous bathtub

17 c) All of these and more

18 a) The Giraffe

19 b) A fish-monger

20 c) Both a) and b)

21 a) Billy

22 a) He was an expert on the animals of Africa

23 a) To put Duke in good humour

24 b) He carried him in his huge beak

25 c) Furry bits of wire

26 b) He did a jiggly dance and sang a song — 'We are the Window-Cleaners'

27 b) Were starving, famished and perishing with hunger

28 a) The Duke of Hampshire

29 b) 'They'll keep us going for ever!'

30 c) Stealing them

31 a) The Giraffe's Magical Neck — it could stretch right into the clouds

32 b) They saw a thief in one of the rooms — the bedroom

33 c) A super-sharp sword

34 b) Billy in the Pelly's beak

35 a) He was shouting at the gardener

36 a) His beak is the bucket that holds the water

37 c) Both a) and b)

38 c) Six hundred and seventy-seven — not counting the greenhouse

39 c) To pick his apples in the autumn

40 c) He thought the Giraffe couldn't reach

41 b) He hadn't seen out of his windows for forty years

42 b) A revolver went off inside his beak

43 c) The Cobra — the cleverest and most dangerous cat-burglar in the world!

44 c) To own the Grubber

45 a) The Rainbow Drops which let you spit in seven different colours

46 a) Glumptious Globgobblers with all the juices of Arabia

47 c) Devil's Drenchers that set your breath on fire

48 b) The Monkey

49 c) He could give the Duke a ride in his beak

50 c) An invitation to clean windows

51 b) They gave him the juicy cherries

52 a) He was the Business Manager

53 a) The chauffeur patched it the same way he patched the tyre of the Rolls-Royce

54   b) He gave them a home on his Estate, with every comfort they desired

55   b) Scarlet Scorchdroppers from Iceland, guaranteed to keep you warm

56   c) A book — it is always there to be opened whenever you wish to meet all your friends again

57   a) Pelly with his Marvellous Beak

Matilda

1   *a) Wormwood*

2   *c) Great Expectations*

3   *a) A car dealer*

4   *c) Because she was good at sums*

5   *b) Miss Trunchbull*

6   *b) Miss Honey*

7   *b) Pigtails*

8   *a) Her mathematical ability*

9   *b) One with no children in it*

10   *c) Agatha*

11   *b) Mrs Phelps*

12   *c) Superglue*

13   *c) A limerick*

14   *A bad girl — they were much harder to squash*

15   *c) To tell them Matilda was a brilliant child*

16   *c) Putting a stinkbomb under her desk*

17   *b) Hortensia*

18   *b) Her hairstyle*

19   *All of them*

20   *b) She makes a song about them*

21   *b) Small people*

22   *b) Matilda*

23   *c) In a tiny cottage*

24   *b) Play bingo*

25   *c) Platinum blonde hair-dye*

26   *b) Mrs Wormwood*

27   *b) He was eating sweets in class*

28   *b) He stole Miss Trunchbull's slice of cake*

29   *b) She forced him to eat an enormous chocolate cake*

30   b) Lavender

31   a) Rupert

32   b) She lifted him up by the hair

33   a) A spray for getting rid of small children

34   a) When she got angry – at small children

35   a) She toppled the glass of water and the newt over Miss Trunchbull

36   b) She ate margarine

37   c) Wilfred

38   b) Michael

39   b) Mr Wormwood

40   c) A lock-up cupboard in Miss Trunchbull's office

41   a) When Hortensia poured a tin of Golden Syrup on the Trunchbull's chair

42   b) She knocked his front teeth out

43   b) Because he succeeded in eating the cake

44   c) What

45   c) Its engine fell out

46   b) Miss Honey

47   b) On a glass of water

48   b) Magnus

49   b) She wrote on the board with chalk

50   b) In front of the telly

51   a) An athlete – she threw the hammer for Britain in the Olympics

52   b) Miss Trunchbull

53   b) Miss Trunchbull took all her salary

54   b) She was now using all her brains in the top form

55   b) She fainted

56   b) Because Matilda's dad was wanted by the police

57   a) She forged her father's will

58   a) The Red House

59   b) Miss Trunchbull murdered him

60   b) With Miss Honey

THE BFG

Just imagine suddenly knowing you may be eaten for breakfast in the very near future; dropped like a rasher of bacon into a frying pan sizzling with fat.

This is exactly what worries Sophie when she is snatched from her bed in the middle of the night by a giant with a stride as long as a tennis court. Luckily for Sophie, the BFG is far more jumbly than his disgusting neighbours, whose favourite pastime is guzzling and swallomping nice little chiddlers. Sophie is determined to stop all this and so she and the BFG cook up an ingenious plan to rid the world of groggle-humping, bog-thumping giants for ever!

THE WITCHES

Witches don't even look like witches. They don't ride round on broomsticks. They don't even wear black cloaks and hats. They are vile, despicable, scheming harridans who disguise themselves as nice, ordinary ladies.

So how can you tell when you're face to face with one? Read this story and you'll find out all you need to know. You'll also meet a real hero, a wise old grandmother and the most gruesome, grotesque gang of witches imaginable!